CHRISTMAS POEMS

Christmas Poems

by

WENDY COPE

Illustrated by
Michael Kirkham

FABER & FABER

First published in 2017
by Faber & Faber Ltd
Bloomsbury House
74–77 Great Russell Street
London WC1B 3DA

Typeset by Faber & Faber Ltd
Printed in Europe

A CIP record for this book is available
from the British Library

ISBN 978–0–571–33858–0

4 6 8 10 9 7 5 3

~

Acknowledgements

Some of these poems first appeared in the *Observer*, the *Spectator* and the *Daily Telegraph*, and are included in earlier books by Wendy Cope.

'A Christmas Poem' was commissioned by the Canadian Broadcasting Corporation. 'Bethlehem' was commissioned by Winchester College to be set to music by Charles Mauleverer.

Other poems have been set by the following composers: Marcus Tristan Heathcock ('A Christmas Song'), Jools Holland ('A Christmas Song'), Beresford King-Smith ('The Christmas Life'), Sasha Johnson Manning ('The Christmas Life'), Roxanna Panufnik ('The Christmas Life'), Richard Percy ('The Christmas Life', 'Another Christmas Poem'), Martin Read ('The Christmas Life', 'A Christmas Poem').

~

Contents

CHRISTMAS POEMS

A Christmas Poem

At Christmas little children sing and merry bells
      jingle,

The cold winter air makes our hands and faces
      tingle

And happy families go to church and cheerily they
      mingle

And the whole business is unbelievably dreadful,
      if you're single.

~

Christmas Ornaments

The mice attacked the Holy Family –
The one I bought in Prague, made out of straw.
By Christmas, Joseph was an amputee
And Mary and the baby were no more.
But I have other treasures to display –
Two perching birds, a Santa Claus, a clown,
A rooster from the church in Santa Fé,
A little harp and drum, a shoe, a crown –
Collected in the years I've lived with you,
The years of warmth and love and Christmas trees,
And someone to come home to, someone who
Can share what I bring back from overseas
And sometimes travel with me. Darling, look –
Our moon from Paris, glittering on its hook.

~

Little Donkey

The children's favourite. We had
to sing it in the Christmas concert
every year, plodding along
with me at the piano, and a child
going clip-clop with coconut shells
or woodblock: a coveted job.

It wasn't my favourite.
After I left teaching
I forgot about it
for more than ten years

until one day, near Christmas,
in a busy high street
a Salvation Army band
began to play it. I stood still

with tears in my eyes.
Little Donkey. All those children
who loved it so much.
All those hands in the air
begging to be chosen
to make the sound of his hooves.

~

A Christmas Song

Why is the baby crying
On this, his special day,
When we have brought him lovely gifts
And laid them on the hay?

He's crying for the people
Who greet this day with dread
Because somebody dear to them
Is far away or dead,

For all the men and women
Whose love affairs went wrong,
Who try their best at merriment
When Christmas comes along,

For separated parents
Whose turn it is to grieve
While children hang their stockings up
Elsewhere on Christmas Eve,

For everyone whose burden,
Carried through the year,
Is heavier at Christmastime,
The season of good cheer.

That's why the baby's crying
There in the cattle stall:
He's crying for those people.
He's crying for them all.

~

O Come, All Ye Faithful

Born the King of Angels —
That's the bit drives music teachers
Round the bend. 'It's An-gels.
Two notes. Not A-an-gels.'
I've fought some battles
With that extra note
And still get wound up every Christmas.

Daddy had a different problem
With the same hymn.
Sing all ye citizens
Of Heaven above.
'Heaven', he asserted,
'Is not a city.
It should be *denizens*.'

And that was what he sang.
It wasn't too embarrassing
But I can't sing the verse
Without remembering. In recent years
I have paid tribute to his memory
By singing, rather quietly,
'Denizens of Heaven above.'

King of an - gels!
flesh ap - pear - ing!
in the high - est!

e, let us a -

~

Bethlehem

There stands a church in Bethlehem today,
Built where the baby in the manger lay,
Where Mary touched and kissed his little face:
A place of pilgrimage, a holy place.

O holy Jesus, Everlasting Light,
Let there be peace in Bethlehem tonight.

And once, in better times, I travelled there,
Watched children run around in Manger Square,
Then went into the church's crypt and stood
Before the birthplace of the Son of God.

O holy Jesus, Everlasting Light,
Let there be peace in Bethlehem tonight.

Now, in the little town where Christ was born,

Young men and children die, and mothers mourn.

Wise men have not brought peace to Manger
Square.

O hear us as we offer up this prayer:

O holy Jesus, Everlasting Light,
Let there be peace in Bethlehem tonight.

~

The Christmas Life

*If you don't have a real tree, you don't bring
the Christmas life into the house.*
— JOSEPHINE MACKINNON, AGED 8

Bring in a tree, a young Norwegian spruce,
Bring hyacinths that rooted in the cold.
Bring winter jasmine as its buds unfold —
Bring the Christmas life into this house.

Bring red and green and gold, bring things
    that shine,
Bring candlesticks and music, food and wine.
Bring in your memories of Christmas past.
Bring in your tears for all that you have lost.

Bring in the shepherd boy, the ox and ass,
Bring in the stillness of an icy night,
Bring in a birth, of hope and love and light.
Bring the Christmas life into this house.

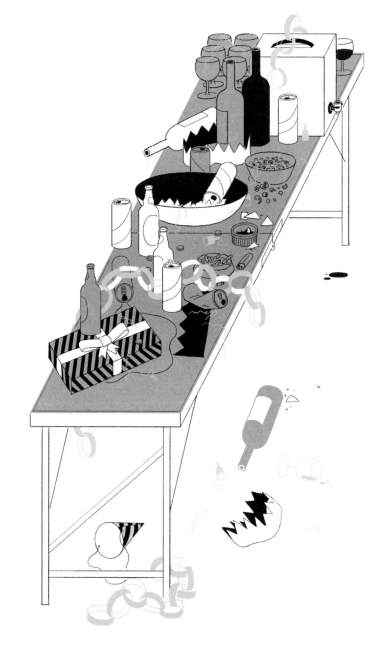

~

Christmas Triolet

for Gavin Ewart

It's Christmas, season of wild bells
And merry carols. On the floor
Are gifts in pretty paper shells.
It's Christmas, season of wild Belle's
Big party. George's stomach swells
With ale; his wife's had even more.
It's Christmas, season of wild belles,
And merry Carol's on the floor.

~

Motorway Music

At last, in spite of everything,
The moment does arrive.
This year it was on Christmas Eve,
Teatime, M25,

When I switched on the radio
And heard 'Nowell, Nowell',
And had to join in, singing for
The King of Israel,

Along with half the choirs on earth
And all the choirs of Heaven,
As I drove through the pouring rain,
Approaching Junction 7.

And then my passenger woke up
And came in with his bass.
I wanted to see happiness
Like ours on every face

In every car. The traffic slowed.
The queue went on and on.
The sound of trumpets introduced
Another Christmas song.

Who cares about a traffic jam
While herald angels sing?
Each year the moment does arrive,
In spite of everything.

~

Christmas Cards

Cards to the very old
go out like doves
who will bring back news
of one kind or another.

It may be a sign of life —
a few sentences
in a shaky hand,
I hope that you are well.

It may be a letter
from a friend or relative
who found my address on the back:
I am very sorry to tell you . . .

This year two cards,
both to widowers,
came winging back with labels:
Addressee gone away.

I open my Christmas list,
find their names
and type *d.2016.*
I could remove them

but that would leave
no trace of them
and I am not quite ready
for them to disappear.

Cathedral Carol Service

Those of us who are not important enough
To have places reserved for us,
And who turned up too late to get a seat at all,
Stand in the nave aisles, or perch on stone ledges.

We shiver in the draught from the west door.
We cannot see the choir, the altar or the candles.
We can barely see the words on our service sheets.

But we can hear the music. And we can sing
For the baby whose parents were not important
        enough
To have a place reserved for them,
And who turned up too late to get a room at all.

~

Another Christmas Poem

Bloody Christmas, here again.
Let us raise a loving cup:
Peace on earth, goodwill to men,
And make them do the washing-up.

~

Note on the Author and Illustrator

Wendy Cope was born in Erith, Kent. After university she worked for fifteen years as a primary-school teacher in London. Her first collection of poems, *Making Cocoa for Kingsley Amis*, was published in 1986 and her most recent, *Family Values*, in 2011. In 1987 she received a Cholmondeley Award for poetry and in 1995 the American Academy of Arts and Letters Michael Braude Award. *Two Cures for Love: Selected Poems 1979–2006* was published in 2008.

Michael Kirkham is an illustrator who has worked for many international clients, including Google, the *New Yorker*, the *New York Times* and the Folio Society. He lives in Edinburgh with his partner and their two children.

~

Note on the Type

This edition is printed in Centaur type, designed by Bruce Rogers (1870–1957). The type takes its name from a book designed by Rogers for publication in 1915, *The Centaur* by Maurice de Guérin, and draws its inspiration from Nicolas Jenson's Humanist designs in Venice, around 1470. It is frequently regarded as among the most attractive Roman revivals of the twentieth century, and had its most notable use in Rogers's own design for the folio edition of the Oxford Lectern Bible, begun in 1929 and published in 1935.

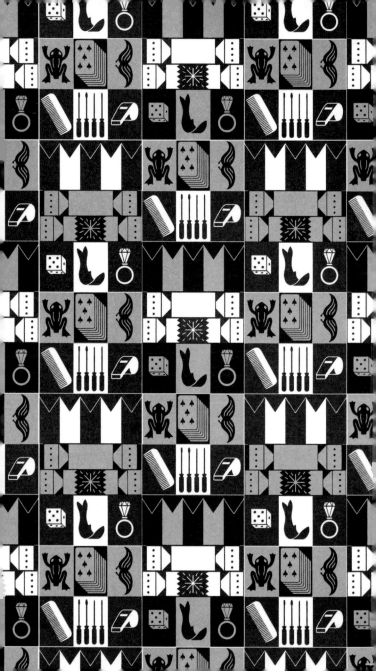